Animal
Faces
At Night

Hannah Kate Sackett

Illustrated by Martin Camm

 **Children's Publishing**

Columbus, Ohio

This edition published in the United States in 2003 by
Waterbird Books,
an imprint of McGraw-Hill Children's Publishing,
A Division of The McGraw-Hill Companies
8787 Orion Place
Columbus, Ohio 43240-4027

www.MHkids.com

Library of Congress Cataloging-in-Publication Data is on file with the publisher.

Created and produced by Firecrest Books Ltd.
in association with Martin Camm.

Art and Editorial Direction by Peter Sackett
Edited by Norman Barrett
Edited in the U.S. by Joanna Callihan
U.S. Production by Nathan Hemmelgarn
Designed by Phil Jacobs
Color Separation by SC International Pte Ltd, Singapore

Printed and bound in Dubai.

ISBN 1-57768-427-3

1 2 3 4 5 6 7 8 9 10 FBL 06 05 04 03

Contents

White Rhinoceros

As the sun sets and the air cools, the white rhinoceros stirs and rises to its feet. It walks across the African plains, nibbling or grazing at the grass as it goes. Its wide, flat lips help the white rhino grab hold of the short grass. The white rhino has two large horns on its nose. These horns are made from a material similar to hair. The larger of the two horns is usually around 24 inches long, but can be longer. The rhino uses its horns to defend itself against animals like hyenas and lions that hunt at night.

Oilbird

As darkness falls, many nocturnal animals, or animals that are active at night, stir from their sleep. In South America, the oilbird emerges from the pitch-black cave it roosts in during the day to look for food. This bird commonly eats fruit. The oilbird uses its strong beak to pull fruit from the trees, then swallows the fruit whole. The oilbird makes high-pitched clicking sounds that echo off of hard objects such as trees and cave walls. Scientists think that oilbirds navigate by listening to these echoes.

Fruit Bat

Like oilbirds, many bats rely on their sense of hearing to find their way at night. Other bats, like the fruit bat, rely on their good eyesight and excellent sense of smell. During the day, large numbers of fruit bats hang upside-down among the trees of southern Asia and Africa. They wake up at dusk to search for food and use their sense of smell to find the fruits that make up their diet. These bats have peg-like teeth that are used to crush fruit. Fruit bats swallow the fruit juice and spit out the seeds and flesh.

Kiwi

The kiwi is another animal with a keen sense of smell. This is unusual for a bird. Found only in New Zealand, the kiwi has nostrils at the very end of its long beak. It also has tiny wings, but cannot fly. Once the sun sets, the kiwi moves about, sniffing around the forest undergrowth for food. It uses its beak to turn over bark and fallen leaves in search of worms, seeds, and berries. It also stirs up the soil looking for insects, which it quickly catches and eats.

Aardvark

The aardvark has a long nose and large nostrils that it uses to sniff out ants and termites. Once the aardvark has found a termite mound or anthill, it digs into the nest. While it is digging, the long hairs around its nostrils close together. This stops dirt from going up its nose. The aardvark catches its tiny prey with its long, sticky tongue. At night, its large ears point forward, helping the aardvark sense its way through the darkness.

Fennec Fox

The fennec is a small fox with very large ears. Its excellent sense of hearing helps the fennec track its prey—lizards, insects, and birds—in the dark. The fennec's ears also help it stay cool in the hot desert. Their large surface area cools its blood as it passes through this part of its body. The fennec has large eyes to help it see when there is very little light. Many nocturnal animals share this feature.

Aye-Aye

One of the strangest nighttime animals is the aye-aye. The aye-aye is a very rare and endangered monkey-like creature that lives only in the rain forests of Madagascar, a country in Africa. At night, the aye-aye relies on its large eyes to search the trees for food. It then uses its large ears to listen for the sound of insect larvae feeding inside the tree trunk. When it hears movement, the aye-aye rips away the bark with its strong teeth to get to the larvae inside. Its teeth are so powerful they can break through the thick shell of a coconut, a food that makes up its diet.

Jaguar

This big cat of South America often hunts by climbing trees and waiting in the darkness for its prey to pass below. The jaguar uses its sharp teeth to catch its prey, including large rodents, called capybaras, and pig-like peccaries. Like other cats, the jaguar has eyes that reflect light, allowing it to see well at night. The dark spots on the jaguar's face and body help it to blend into the shadows, so it can hunt its prey without being seen.

Tasmanian Devil

Another nocturnal animal is the Tasmanian devil. Found only on the Australian island of Tasmania, the Tasmanian devil has powerful jaws and teeth that allow it to eat every scrap of its prey. When threatened, it opens its mouth wide to show its teeth. Its ears turn from pale pink to a deep red. The Tasmanian devil earned the name "devil" because of the bizarre noises it makes, ranging from snorts, snarls, and coughs to blood-curdling shrieks.

Gecko

The tokay gecko, a large lizard found in southeast Asia, was named after the noise it makes. Only males make this bark, which sounds like "tokeh" or "gekoh." Scientists think this sound is used to attract females. The gecko has large, bulging, yellow eyes to help it see at night. Two clear eyelids that are joined together protect the eyes. The gecko's large, flat head and wide jaws are designed to catch insects, mice, and other lizards. The tokay gecko is thought by some to bring good luck.

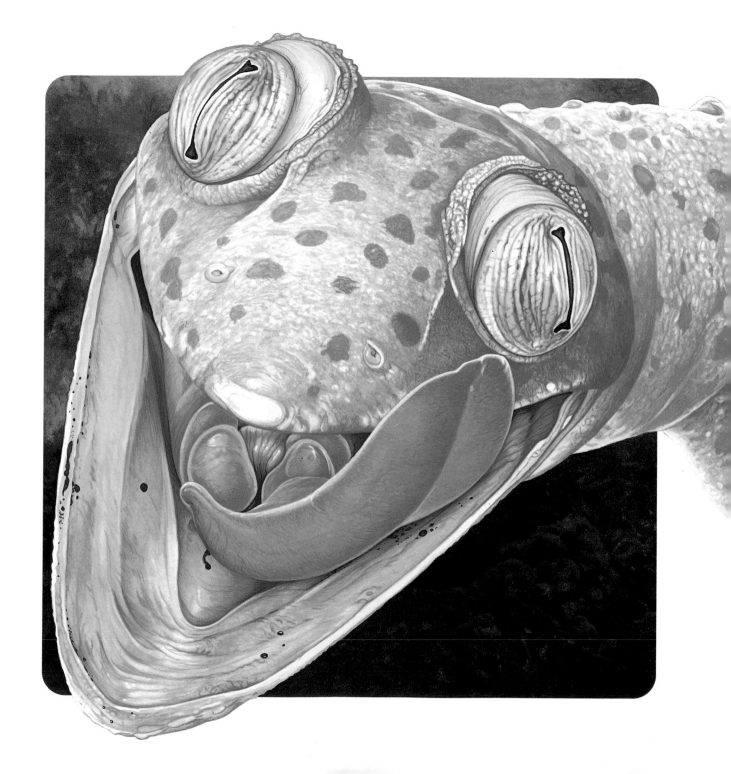

House Mouse

The house mouse is a nighttime animal that commonly visits people's homes. Instead of eating insects, this mouse is more likely to find its meals in cupboards or on kitchen shelves. Its large, flat, sharp-edged front teeth help the mouse chew through cardboard and wood to get to food. The house mouse can even chew through leather or tear up cloth to make a nest. It has good hearing but weak eyesight. The house mouse uses its long whiskers, which are highly sensitive to touch, to find its way in the dark. Many other animals, such as cats, use whiskers in the same way.

Catfish

The catfish is named for its whiskery features, which give it the appearance of a cat. The whiskers are sense organs, called barbels. The barbels are equipped with taste organs that help the catfish find food in dark waters. The European catfish (right) has long barbels on the upper part of its face and shorter ones beneath its chin. The American bullhead (below) has hornlike barbels above its mouth. Some Asian catfish have barbels that look like worms. The catfish lure their prey into their mouth with these wormlike barbels.

Luna Moth

The long sensors on the head of a moth are called antennae. Antennae help the moth locate the source of a smell. Some moths have smooth, narrow antennae. The luna moth has feathery antennae that are especially sensitive. Male luna moths use their sharp sense of smell to follow scents given off by female moths. Unlike most moths, the luna moth only eats when it is a caterpillar, or larva. Because the luna moth does not eat, it only lives for about one week. The luna moth has four spots on its pale green wings, called eyespots. Scientists think that these eyespots scare off predators, such as birds, who may perceive the spots as the eyes of a larger animal.

Facts Behind the Faces

The animals in this book are all nocturnal, which means they are active at night or in the dim light of dusk and dawn. Large eyes, large ears, and a keen sense of smell help many of them find their way in the darkness. This part of the book tells you more about these animals—where they live, their relatives, their eating habits, and their enemies. From the wide-eyed aye-aye to the long-nosed aardvark, here are the facts behind the faces.

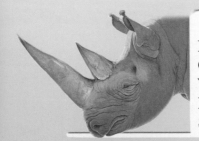

White Rhinoceros
Family: The white rhinoceros is one of five kinds of rhinoceros.
Other rhinoceroses: Indian, Javan, Sumatran, and black rhinos.
Where they live: Northeastern and southern Africa.
Enemies: Human beings hunt them for their horns and skin.
Size: Around 6 feet tall, can weigh up to 5,000 pounds.

Oilbird
Family: The oilbird is the only animal in its family.
Where they live: Warm, northern regions of Latin America.
What they eat: Fruit, especially of palms and laurels.
Size: Around 17 inches in length.
Special features: The fat of oilbirds was once used as cooking and lamp oil.

Fruit Bat
Family: There are around 160 members of the fruit bat family.
Other bats: Vampire bats, brown bats, and pipistrelle bats.
Where they live: Asia and Africa.
Size: Its wingspan can be as much as 5 feet, like the great gray owl.
Special features: Much like bees, fruit bats pollinate plants and flowers.

Kiwi

Family: There are three different kiwis in the kiwi family.
Related birds: Ostrich, rhea, emu, and cassowary.
Where they live: Only in New Zealand.
Enemies: Dogs, ferrets, and human beings.
Special features: It has tiny wings and cannot fly.

Aardvark

Family: The aardvark is the only member of its family.
Where they live: Across Africa, except for the northern deserts.
What they eat: Ants and termites.
Enemies: Lions and human beings hunt them for food.
Size: Up to 5 feet in length.

Fennec Fox

Family: The fennec fox is a member of the dog family.
Other foxes: Red, kit, arctic, and bat-eared foxes.
Where they live: The deserts of northern Africa and northern Arabia.
What they eat: Lizards, birds, insects, rodents, eggs, and plants.
Size: Only 14-17 inches in length, its ears can be as long as 6 inches.

Aye-Aye

Family: The aye-aye is a primate, and the only member of its family.
Other primates: Apes, monkeys, and human beings.
Where they live: They are found only in Madagascar.
What they eat: Insects, eggs, and coconuts.
Enemies: Human beings because they are destroying their habitat.

Jaguar

Family: The jaguar is a member of the cat family.
Other large cats: Leopard, lion, tiger, and cheetah.
Where they live: North, South, and Central America.
What they eat: Capybaras, peccaries, deer, sheep, birds, and fish.
Size: 5-6 feet in length, 150-300 pounds in weight.

Tasmanian Devil
Family: Marsupials—animals born in an extremely young state.
Related marsupials: Kangaroo, dunnart, and tiger quoll.
Where they live: Only on the Australian island of Tasmania.
What they eat: Almost anything, including kangaroos and wombats.
Size: Around 3 feet long and up to 22 pounds in weight.

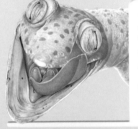

Gecko
Family: The tokay gecko is one of around 700 geckos.
Other geckos: Leopard, marbled, and leaf-tailed geckos.
Where they live: South America, southern Asia, Florida, and Texas.
What they eat: Insects, spiders, small lizards, birds, and mice.
Size: 11-14 inches in length.

House Mouse
Family: The house mouse is a member of the rodent family.
Other rodents: Rat, vole, harvest mouse, grasshopper mouse, and gerbil.
Where they live: Originally from Asia, now across most of the world.
What they eat: Grain, plants, meat, and seeds.
Enemies: Human beings, cats, dogs, owls, foxes, snakes, and rats.

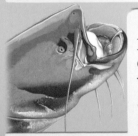

Catfish
Family: There are around 2,000 kinds of catfish.
Other catfish: Bullheads, royal catfish, electric catfish, and walking catfish.
Where they live: Throughout the world.
Size: Up to 16 feet in length, can weigh over 400 pounds.
Special features: Some have spines on their back that give off poison.

Luna Moth
Family: The luna moth is part of the giant silkworm and royal moth family.
Similar moths: Indian moon and Madagascan comet moths.
Where they live: North America.
What they eat: Nothing, but as caterpillars they eat tree leaves.
Size: Wingspan of 4-5 inches.

Index